*Wilson Wiley
Variations*

Poems

Thoreau Lovell

Wet Cement Press
Berkeley, California

Copyright© 2019 Thoreau Lovell
All rights reserved

ISBN: 978-1-7324369-1-6

Wet Cement Press
Berkeley, California

www.wetcementpress.com

wetcementpress@gmail.com

Cover drawing by Sheridan Jones,
a self-portrait artist and photographer living
in the Cotswolds in the United Kingdom.

Deepest thanks to the many close friends and
acquaintances who have inspired these poems
and helped them along. Especially to John
High, cryptic and loving poet-monk, for his
subtle and continuous support.

WCP2-1

Contents

Wilson Wiley Variations, Part One
- Raised in Name's Light — 1
- Number 9 Dream — 2
- Hiding Out in Desire — 6
- Dust Headed South — 8
- Yodel — 10

Some Perfect Impossible California
- The Gardener's Wife — 15
- Twenty Naked Pentecostals — 17
- One Letter Separates Us — 18
- So Late In the History of Souls — 19
- Inside the Glossy Heart of Language — 20
- Mudflats Home Bay — 21
- Wonder Pond — 22
- Eating the Same Fruit that Made Mother Crazy
    - 1. Potential Birds — 25
    - 2. The Thin Blade of Her Face — 26
    - 3. If an Angel Came — 27
- Under a Weed-Puller's Gaze — 28
- The People-Packed Hills — 29
- Music Simple as Standing There — 30
- After Talking Long Distance to a Minneapolis Cab Driver — 31

The Devil Writes Books in a White Shirt and Bright Green Tie

- The Gate of Measure and Desire — 35
- Everyone Still Awake Wants to get Married — 37
- Small Oval Mirrors — 39
- Scissoring Her Song — 41
- The City of Sand — 44

Strange Way to Grow Old

- Autumn for A — 49
- Walking at Villa Montalvo — 50
- Drinking Wine with the Ancestors — 51
- Thunderheads — 52
- The Professor's Lament — 53
- A Dream — 54
- Quilt Writing — 56

Wilson Wiley Variations, Part Two

- The Last Mile Away — 61
- Gone as Water — 66
- Apotheosis of Childhood — 67
- Memory's Continuous Ragtime — 68
- The Harmonica Kettle's Sad Drone — 69
- The Edge of Contentment — 70
- Another Charlie Chaplin Heart Attack — 71
- The Vat-like Valley — 72
- A Book Called Forgetting — 74

About the Author — 77

Wet Cement Press Titles — 79

The trick is to be literal-minded in the world of multiple metaphor, and fabulous in the face of the literal.

—*Charles Simic*

Wilson Wiley Variations, Part One

Raised in Name's Light

Haze-screened mountains shimmer above
the valley floor. Mother scratching

the outline of a letter that becomes home.
An illegible page between skin and sky.

Between each letter, expectation, sticky meaning,
a familiar shape distorted, debased. Her
cramped hand, metallic surf, smoky kisses.

Pointing at every simultaneous thing
that splits Wilson from Wiley. And
raises him in Name's light.

Fig trees in retreat. Bits of cotton.
Broken rhythm. One foot running,
one foot numb and dragging.

How does one escape the need to escape?
Wilson asks Wiley. The grave, says Wiley.
Father dirt. The auditorium of the soul.
Electricity and stars reversed in the sky.

Wilson hears a long-dying melody. Says nothing
about resemblance. Water pooling underground.

Name and Wilson. Wiley and Name.
Electric guitars are to blame.

Number 9 Dream

Ax-blue winter
where they stop for the night.

Wilson argues the water
is well or wonder. In a tiny cabin
in the New Mexico Night.

Cold as number 12.

Sex is a faucet and pipes, a civilized
tangle of pipes and valves open at both ends.

Sex is number 11.

The Woman-Who-Comes-and-Goes
embraces the fake frontier.

Albuquerque south, the bloom
of its urban underwebbing.

Thanks, Jack, for the broken-hearted rodeo.
The dry grass and cotton candy alias.

The W-W-C-and-G remembers.

Her radio it's number 10.

Mesa Verde north the 4 neat corners
west and north.

Follow, Wiley says, the blue groin
closed like the hard fist the mountain
holds above the cabin roof.

Bullet holes. Rocks in your new boots.
The cattle of memory.

For the new year number 9.

Wilson says love dear don't follow,
rose petals in his suitcase,
he says love don't follow it leads.

The Black Heart is number 8.
The Steel Thumb number 7.

He remembers her body in icy water.
The handle the trigger inky blue.

Number 6 is the walking dream.

The New Mexico Night unfurls a fence
across the sky. Each star a barb
between heaven and earth.

The New Mexico Night is number 5.

A tiny cabin is warmth and biscuits.
The tongue-lapping choreography
of flame on wood.

Wilson watches Wiley burn.
A portrait of a mountain range on the wall.
Wilson watches the portrait burn.

The Woman-Who-Comes-And-Goes
writes that regret is like a pair of handcuffs.

The act of possession is number 4.

She counts on another body to fill her
as a landscape fills space. Mountains
of frozen rock and snow. Each tree
a potential suitor. Each trail a lover's spine.

She counts her wits as her compass.

The art of escape is number 3.

Two lovers sit in a field of snow.
Breathing a warm rope between them.

A hawk dives, plunges, rips and tears.
Driven by possession.

Their breathing stops, their speaking stops,
their bodies stop, their thinking stops.

Lovers strip old carrots for the stew.

Blood-warmth is number 2.
Number 1 is shape's persistent stare.

Wilson hides in the trunk
with the potatoes and the gun.

Woman-Whose voice echoes
through the cold dark room.

Jack, drunken Jack, counts the hairs
on his lover's chest.

Beneath the silver-dollar eye of the moon.

Hiding Out in Desire

At the moment of creation, Wiley's desire
is music that snaps time's step.

A) If he pulls out a gun and shoots his father
he takes a new name.

B) Of all the countries in the world, not of any.

His single-hatted self made multiple.
Handclaps ricocheting through
the darkened room.

Shrill, grating voices, smoothed together.
O moon too empty for words.
This rhythmic lie.

Radio and television, short wave and satellite,
canceling news struck by tongue.

Wiley starts out where truck-rust turns
water red. Escaping with his stolen name.

A) If he gives her an apple, she is the organic
source of his passion.

B) If the father refuses to die, the genre
is slapstick horror.

A wobbly blue shade fleeing gray
as memory flees the small fire
Wiley's necessity makes.

No place is place enough for Wiley.

He sits very still and shakes his written head
like a ragged melody in the wind.

Wiley wants degrees of black broadcast
across the sky. He wants to want.

Hiding out in desire
keeping it close to his skin
for the long sea voyage crossing.

A) Of all the lies to be told, why this one?

B) A mountain Name piles up over time.

Wiley would gladly exchange his body
for her stories of bravery and good bread.

His mother is water. She's muddy ground.

What love, reads Wiley,
at the moment of creation?

Then all the doors blow open.

Dust Headed South

Wilson hears, but forgets to answer.

His old feedback-tinged guitar
meanders through the valley.

His binoculars spot dust headed south.

A slow-blooded creature nearly spent on optimism.
Moving with the beauty of an old shoe.

Wilson follows.

Autonomous sandstone angels crisscross,
form an altar.

Blue shadows touch Wilson's face
with the smell of rain.

Warm air rushes out of a fist-sized hole
in the ground.

Wiley is Wilson's animal voucher.

He flirts with cylinder and barrel,
cock and bone.

Wiley's grease and percussion bass line.

His upturned nipple.

Mountains return after a giant hand
scooped them flat. Mountains again.

Crisp fried fish. Bones with grass
flowing through.

A maze of blue air.

Wilson wants Wiley's sharpness to enter him.

His silver coins.

His steel strings.

Wilson listens to Wiley sing.

Wiley sings and sings and sings.

Yodel

Them worried blues got no heart to cry.
Them windy, worried, got no.
Them cold-bone, windy, worried, waiting, why.

Then Yodel throws dirt in the face of the sun.
Says I'll not be strangled by anyone.
Yodel always twice your age.

Long road no matter where you begin
or end it, says Old Man Yodel,
dealt a two-cent ace, one-eyed queen,
a mismatch of children.

Or that Walking Woman Yodel,
saying I am no more tired of walking
than the earth is tired of making sand.

With a yappy dog tied to a tree,
taught to bark by a boy trying to sing.
But dog's howl is just a four-legged,
fur-blooded Yodel.

And if Guitar is a constellation
in the American sky, then Yodel
is the space between the stars.

And if Guitar is Yodel's coffin,
why don't Yodel ever close his eyes?

The highway makes for a long black rainbow
with an empty guitar case at either end,
a crow marking every remembered mile,
says Beer-Bottle Yodel.

Them worried blues got no heart to cry.
Them windy, worried, got no.
Them cold-bone, windy, worried, waiting, why.

ically drawn, rubbed away, or pulled apart into a forest of black lines. Watching her felt like watching something private and essential at once: I'd stand by the table for what seemed like hours, not speaking, not breathing too loud, because even the smallest sound might break the spell.

Whatever we couldn't afford my mother found ways to compensate for. Books I couldn't buy, she borrowed from the library and copied passages into notebooks for me. If I mentioned a film at school she hadn't seen, she'd walk me through its story based on other movies she knew. When I pointed at a dress in a store window, she'd note it down and try to sew something close to it at home. Her imitations were never exact, never as good as the real thing, but they carried their own kind of honesty—they said, *I couldn't give you this, but I gave you what I could.*

And yet there were moments when even her resourcefulness failed. I remember standing in the lobby of a theater, watching other children pour through the doors with their parents, each carrying a little bag of popcorn that smelled of butter and salt. My mother knelt beside me and said, very gently, that tonight was not the night. I didn't cry. I had already learned that crying in public made her face change in a way I didn't like, as though some small door inside her was being forced shut. Instead I held her hand and pretended I did not care. Later, at home, she made popcorn on the stove and told me a story about a theater where the screen stretched from one side of the sky to the other, and I told myself this was better.

The Gardener's Wife

The gardener's wife walks down the gravel path that bisects the enormous lawn, ignoring the classical stone sculptures—beautiful young women in robes, frozen snakes, leafy basins without water or reflection. She looks over her shoulder, smiles once, then climbs up the lower branches of a sweeping cypress.

The gardener pushes his hands through the bottoms of his pockets. He remembers a suburban childhood set against a brick mansion. A year of afternoons among saxifrage and common myrtle. A day spent chasing her up the stairs of the villa.

Now, with her spinning hands, the speed of fortune's long legs, she's vanished into the branches of a tree he thinks he taught her the name of.

She tried to tell him. On the driveway. On the veranda. The gardener stands on the lawn, his mouth slowly opening. (Two green, shimmering, ruby-throated hummingbirds dart out of the cypress.)

Every window of the villa swings open, every door that reminds him she's part of the moving landscape. Smoke escaping through a chimney.

He calls out to her, with his slow hands cupped ship-like. Feeling storm pressure build, as inside a big tree—his English Elm.

One day she told him, you think we live on a planet that can invent home forever, and sang it like a curse. Everywhere beyond him. Nowhere outside him.

He waits for her on the porch. A sliver of moon in the darkening sky. Squirrels scamper back and forth beneath the fountain mimicking her busyness. She who drew the statues as if they were about to burst into flower.

And already coyotes barking in the distance. The "whoo, whoo-whoo" of the Great Horned Owl.

Twenty Naked Pentecostals

for John High

Twenty naked Pentecostals cram into a Pontiac,
cross the Texas border into Louisiana,
and crash into a tree.

Out of the wilderness, their vacant lot,
their quick tents and tambourine screams.
They remind us of hoodlum ghosts.
How they bicker and moan
through uneasy sleep.

We hear the slurred songs of boredom
and fatality, rising above small town
drum rolls, minor-key guitar strangulations.

How the children who stay behind
are done in by the stillness of the air
tightening around them.

We hear a chorus rise from the mud,
moody as a tenor saxophone in the suburbs.
Their bottleneck, steel, thump and roll.
Their dark, love-sick repetitions,
send us running back to California.

You like a stunned bear. Me with my suitcase
and tape recorder in hand.

One Letter Separates Us

for Barbara Roether

She says one letter separates "waiting"
from "writing." As we approach
the autumn equinox.

There's a line of hedges, break of trees,
she has quietly stepped through,
now that she's about to have a child.

I left San Francisco for the spiraling sentence
of black rock desert. To be alone
with the weather, the visible emotion
of the gods. Afraid of the softening body,
the most personal of landscapes.

Feeling that our faces are no longer
part of our bodies, but belong to the world
at large, as moons belong to planets.

Arriving in the dead of night, in a dusty canyon,
with the light of her belly flickering inside me.
The blue moon glowing blind over the hill,
over this scrap of desert.

Her body is a sealed letter. She says
the world cannot touch her.

So Late In the History of Souls

I live on a hill where there used to be goats,
the most human of animals, chewing old glass
and pouch tobacco. When San Francisco was
so small you could map it on the lines of your
hand.

There's bedrock beneath the smell of coffee
roasting and spices mixed and packaged on
the corner. There's an old brewery across
the street and soon a brand new Episcopal
Church will shade the upper yards behind the
empty lot where a small trailer now sits.

I watch a young woman with her feet rubbed
away float up the dirt path between the
red house-barn and a multi-unit apartment
complex. The shrinking woman reaches the
edge of the garden on top of the hill and
stands with her plastic bags of anti-spinach
and manure. The last burst of light exploding
in her smile.

She opens the gate to the community garden.
I sit on a swing that floats over the Mission
and back. Clumps of other people's children
spring up between us.

Inside the Glossy Heart of Language

for Lee Cline

A ragged moss-like ghost floats in the branches
a hundred feet off the ground. Looking through
filtered sunlight. The wind split into endless
rounds of sympathetic singing.

Families enter and exit the park, as in a museum.
Something small and historical. A log cabin,
a logging truck, trucks of gravel and sharp-
tongued drivers. Under a canopy of thought
intercepting sunlight.

This is a place to stand and wish I was a 30-story
redwood tree crashing to the ground on a
stormy evening. An event once heard hundreds
of miles away, now an image multiplying
through time.

Giants falling, systems crumbling, roots left
dangling inside the glossy heart of language.
Wild and inaccessible.

Distracted, free of the dizzying kaleidoscope
of the future, I think of you inside a passing
airplane. A tiny glint of light in the sky, which, if
focused into a beam, would instantly ignite these
clumps of broken branches on which I stand.

Mudflats Home Bay (Point Reyes)

for Naomi Sacks

West of Mt. Vision, walking over gently
rolling downs. Treeless and wind-cropped.
We cross three causeways to sand still warm
under cloudy skies. Then sit facing the slow
curve of shore and water.

The light insistence of your fingers circling
my lips. You say, "close your eyes," stroking my
palm, my uncurling fingers. You say, "imagine
he walks toward us now, from the sandy
mouth of the *estero*. This English sailor who
knows how to squeeze ecstasy from a chill-
wind. He begins to rub my feet, my calf, as
you slowly lift my blue skirt, pull me gently
toward you."

Through red wine. The lazy gray body of
water. You become my fragile Victorian,
my yellow Scotch broom. With schooners
docked at a makeshift pier, picking up the
Point's rich butter.

At last light, we walk back over the rise, above
Home Bay. Where for years, you tell me,
fragments of Ming china have washed up on
the shore.

Wonder Pond

Because the world is not as closed to me as I to it. I throw a stone not at the shimmering surface of Wonder Pond, but straight up at the sapphire sky.

With late afternoon comes the cooling winds, the keening shadows. As the stone reaches its zenith and begins gathering downward speed The Woman-Who-Comes-And-Goes appears on the other side of the pond. The music in her name mimicking the mechanics of nature.

Cattle wander between the pond and ridge line, far to the east. Southern erratics stand as guard boulders, as stone hounds. To the north the sky is blackest. The pop-up stars brightest.

From the pond, you can't look west. It simply isn't there. An immense mirror rises from what should be the western shore. It extends both north and south a great distance then disappears behind the dark curtain of sky.

I wake at pond's edge wrapped in a dirty blanket. Thicket, thicket, bush and berry. And watch a hummingbird an arm's length away startle absence into presence.

The Woman-Who-Comes-and-Goes hands me a chunk of old bread. We watch a tawny cat tighten and spring on a singing cricket.

This experience or another one, the greasy ducks cluck. Fish nibble at the surface, at the point of contact, nearly present.

I watch dirty water start to boil. Daydream about biscuits hand-shaped into animals. Follow the trail that leads to a handprint dusted on stone. The epic sweep of an arm now written over with defiant profanity.

The Woman-Who-Comes-and-Goes cuts our initials into the moonless sky with her flashlight. I sleep in the dusty middle. Not making a sound. A prostrate body to register the tracks of other bodies that move as night moves.

In the afternoon, I prop memory open with a stick, tooth-marked but still stabilizing. To see the stratification of rock wall up close. Myriad small surfaces at every odd angle. Rust-iron oxidation. Patches of soft orange, brushed brown, dusty gray.

Look, she says, I can't take my eyes off you.
You've stumbled on the rocky slope. Snapped
your pretty neck. You're a carcass in motion.
Sinking into the hillside.

The-Woman-Who-Comes-And-Goes leaves
the smell of mud, smell of eucalyptus, behind
her.

I resume my practice with a pencil and a small
blue notebook. Because the world is not as
closed to me as I to it. These weeks at Wonder
Pond.

Eating the Same Fruit
that Made Mother Crazy

San Juan Bautista Suite

1. Potential Birds

Lie close, frail and silent body.
And read the potential birds in the branches.

Come back as bits of story. Outlaw hummingbird,
dependable robin, solemn dove.

Hear the century's slow stomp rumble
inside wooden balconies.

Inside shopkeepers' creased boots.
Hear it reverberate through the rich valley.

Lie with me on a hot summer day
near *the torture gardens and scenic railways.*

Lie with me in a weed-choked field,
with poplars propped against the wind.

Near the raggedy margin of a shallow ditch,
lost in frog-song.

Sing to me about the land.

Italic text: Jack Spicer

2. The Thin Blade of Her Face

Beyond the endless possibilities for fruit orchards, grapes for altar wine, for raising grain, she rolls up the broken road of kings, in a wooden cart, with wooden wheels, put together with wooden pegs. She rolls over large square floor tiles, past the limestone font, the sundial in the garden.

I follow her meander, her thin lips and bright brown eyes. She says, "fiesta," and thirty cowboys and cowgirls appear in procession, performing the Virginia Reel on horseback.

Caught in the snake-like breeze, Good Souls gather in the square wearing capes of rabbit, a blanket, maybe breechcloth, to watch the tick-tick-talking of stories continue to flow over the earth like water.

A whimsy-priest named her children after his philosophers, taught them to sing in his choir. This wooden Madonna with brittle brown skin. Mother of an Indian boy named Plato. Mother of the first pear in California.

This piece is indebted to
"East of the Gabilans" by Marjorie Pierce

3. If an Angel Came (Would it be Like This?)

Beneath the bleached blue horizon, a bony woman—silence inside speech—led me into a simple room. I took shelter in her skinny arms, her twin highways. Like a young man with a bag of graveyard tricks, unable to dig, unable to bury.

Thinking of her fighting forever the hypodermic music of an accordion squeezed through uninterested air, as she cuts across hills stripped of native grasses, battling through saliva, the dark tunnel of the throat, the armored solar plexus, until the black comedy of the slapstick father flashes before her eyes—inhumanly fast and freeway slick.

Now we're both double-loco, with the Mission slumping forward near the edge of the bluff, above the nearly dry river bed. Pressing our lips tightly together, against a backdrop of broadly brushed wheat fields sparked to flame. Waiting for some prior ocean to wash the illuminated cross off Pagan Hill.

A flock of Red-winged Blackbirds stitch their chatter into the wrinkled landscape. We walk past the dilapidated bleachers of an old rodeo, the overgrown vines of a dusty vineyard, with four thousand Indians buried above us.

Under a Weed-Puller's Gaze

Under a weed-puller's gaze, she ran
the bean fields, crossed the soft highway,
eyes shifting upwards to brain, mind down
to hands and feet, out to fists of blackbirds
pounding young almond trees.

She ran through the Hacienda lobby,
through the Armenian market, to the camps
on the edge of town. Ran through the red
house of the Nebraska horse doctor.

Rivers of orange blossom pollen dust
blackening to sludge swirled in the noon sky
behind her.

The People-Packed Hills

for Delia Garcia

Thick fog rolls over the people-packed hills
of San Francisco.

Lanes of sun fire up the gray folds,
illuminating metal edges.

Had I stayed in Fresno I might have become
a crippled drunk in a '64 Chevy Impala
pulling pavement. A neon blur
stretching down Belmont Avenue.
Hot night-end to hot night-end.

I might have wandered irregular ditch banks,
around shopping malls, looking for the hobo
in the fig orchard.

Land-locked in shell of stucco, with no window
and no door in the square horizon.

Sitting in a Chevy Blazer on Blackstone
at the edge of town, waiting.

Music Simple as Standing There
(Listening to the Grateful Dead)

for Katie Vann

T says listen. How they build, expand, build,
at each step the music throbs and tickles.
K winks and frowns.

T turns up the space, spins in his socks,
arms rising still tight from weight, from waiting.

Music simple as standing there he thinks.
And opens his fingers through high lilting
guitar. What he calls, orchestral air.

Or what J, returning from across the sea,
might say, swells. Meaning T feels her
twang and thump.

While K, a sweet dose of live bump and run,
sings the blue horn highway, back turned,
turning away.

T sways, types, retreats, falls.
The dark always crash romance.

And behind him, a mountain silent
and gray, moving through some perfect
impossible California.

After Talking Long Distance to a Minneapolis Cab Driver

for Anthony Schlagel

If the blood of a blood orange drips down
the arms of a skinny woman in back,
if she's nobody's best friend, with breasts
as cold as snowbound hubcaps,
drop her at the intersection of Drunk
or Too-Sober-to-Care, and head out west
of the West.

Once you cross the fiercely unstable Sierras,
every long hour of the mind you spent
getting here returns doubled
in paper-thin sunshine,
or fog that rolls through open windows,
or fresh rain that chills the air
just enough to excite the body awake.

The Devil Writes Books in a White Shirt and Bright Green Tie

The Gate of Measure and Desire

Having entered the city through the gate of *Measure* and *Desire*, the ruined and gentle gate of *Reading* and *Travel*, they meet on a cold stone bench above the crescent shaped bay. Trying to smooth the wobble of the world.

She runs down the winding path feeling lucky as water filling every crevice, she runs through this city of circles, curves and arcs, a city flying through time faster than the landscape that surrounds it. He catches only a flicker of fabric, a whip of her hair as he pushes through the crowd.

Standing alone in a tangle of forest, he imagines both of them dancers. She, with her bad eye, off balance, he with his broken ribs, rousing the sharp earthy wine pressed from the hills, the sinewy mushrooms gathered in the wet creases of the hills, salt that stings like a mosquito's bite.

On the Friday before Feast, the Tuesday before Numbers, he finds her waiting in front of the arch known as *Encouragement*. In front of the butcher paper arch of *Childhood*. Listening for the harsh pluck or strum, suspecting even the simplest music.

Once they leave through the gate of *Ever Widening Hunger*, their future together and apart, they turn and look back at the city, gray and diminishing, fading behind a curtain of spring rain.

Everyone Still Awake Wants to get Married

for John High & Michelle Murphy

She looks at him across the airport bar, a postcard of goats scrapping rocky soil before her on the table, then sets her head down, as if to sleep. She imagines her name in different handwriting, written over every part of her body, as if the perfect signature could lift her out of the airport.

He stands at the bar watching her slumped in a red velvet booth. His red suspenders, red eyes, and rough fingertips. He decides they dream in tandem. That they have followed a silent tattoo of light through a stone doorway, into a small room, where dozens of children are singing in different languages.

The lanky man waits in front of her booth, black pants, a wrinkled blue cap, having recently returned from a gray country, where he saw many buildings padlocked and boarded up with pigeons flying in and out of broken windows.

We barbarians want circuses, an old news-selling woman told him, having dreamt the night before that her husband was the wick

of an enormous candle. We want cigarettes
and beer, an occasional hot meal, just like the
multitudes of worshipers who came before us.

He says he would like to sit inside one of the
circular straw houses clumped around an old
tree in her postcard, talk to the skinny black
man telling stories. She says nothing exists here,
except smoke and billboards, once you leave the
airport. He describes a carless town square at
dusk. A stone angel on a tower.

Could they stay in the airport forever,
together? She asks that question silently
to herself, already entirely at ease with his
stuttering intuition. Knowing he is the wind
and not the trash blowing across the runway.

The bar closes and even the secret bottles are
emptied. Now he can't leave her side, having
found the ragged border between dream and
remembering. Bells sound and telephones ring.
Everyone still awake wants to get married.
Transistor radios stop and static fills the air.

As the sky turns bright purple, a postcard of
elephants storming through an African village
slips from her fingers and falls to the carpeted
floor. They both stand up as if to walk away.
The stranded crowd beautifully ignoring them.

Small Oval Mirrors

for Olga Astafyeva

A Russian woman sits with her back to the window, waiting for space itself to become visible in the small oval mirrors hanging from the ceiling. A candle burns on the bookshelf. On TV, a man and woman in black and white evening clothes dance around an empty table.

Her apartment is surrounded by a birch forest, where men on skis argue about the last war. Time is different here, she tries to tell one of them. Here the devil writes books in a white shirt and bright green tie. Here the soup is always in the fridge.

Give up making your objects, your world of wire mesh and glass, the young man with cold threatening eyes tells her.

She sits down at the wooden table, opens an old book thick with figures peasants have used to keep their horses and dogs alive. She sees the imagination of these animals reflected in the pages of the book.

Soviet-era advertisements repeat themselves on television in the furthest corner of the room.

Her spinning mirrors throw jagged irregularities of light across the dimly lit surface of her face.

What finally appears outside her window—days, weeks, or months later—is a large field of dead grass, full of cardboard boxes and hungry beggars.

Scissoring Her Song

For Nina Iskrenko

1.

Today it's the fat fat robins. The fullness
of breasts disrupting the root of sleep.

She says a silver jet tears a hole in the thin gray sky.
Alphabets tumble down to the busy earth
each attached to a parachute.

She says every musical instrument doubles
a landscape. Every note replaces a body.

She says the soul and the piano are collaborators.
The winds and currents compose a cycle
of songs, the cosmic instability, the many
melodies the clocks sing.

We sit and listen carefully to the piano
as the breeze gives it to us. Cracked open
like a walnut with bolts and weather stripping
and bamboo slivers inserted between the strings.

2.

She says her grandfather was a red-trousered
Bolshevik who traded his name for a clarinet,
a fountain pen, a darkly shaded sentence.

True or false? ask the chrome chimes
hanging from the peach tree.

True or false or family?

3.

I sharpen a pencil.
All my revolutionary ancestors
sharpen their pencils.

4.

It's the erotic of the Moscow subway, she says,
from spine to forest's edge.

The shrill sounds of a toy harmonica.
The quick answer of a ukulele.

A slender mockingbird alights
on a white stovepipe, scissoring her song.

She is our mirror and model. Improvising
and crowing. Squawking at midday,

at midnight, on tall tree-top, floating
on expanded wings, on chimney top,

in door-yard. She's the true harbinger
of nerve wracking transformation!

But who is the irresistible buffoon
left singing in counterfeit moonlight?

The City of Sand

She came over the mountains, across the river, into the city of sand. With the wind always blowing from the west. The clouds constantly streaming overhead.

They meet the very day she arrives. Chance or fortune, a left turn or right, make the necessary addition. As if nature could not abide by the singular.

They stroll in a garden of bright lights and loud music, while the bronze moons flies swiftly through the black sky. They stroll through a city of multiple names, composite faces, a city as relentless as the sun.

At night they lie spine to spine, frame to frame. Mud formed. Laden with. Not desiring a simple love story, a field touched by so many hands.

One day they decide to leave the compact and maze-like city. Because sweet breezes followed the rain and all of the streets inexplicably opened onto the countryside.

She is surprised by how quickly they enter woodland. Green rolling over low hills, stands of oak, sycamore, occasional clumps of pine.

Late in the afternoon, blackbirds swarm low over trees. A living net of flow and agitation, flung from sky to sky. They gather directly overhead, then drop.

The lovers are blinded by the flapping of black wings. Deafened by the raspy hissing of blackbirds. Arms and hands and arms covering faces.

The man and woman can't believe they'll walk no further, now that they have returned to open country. Bringing every fragment of stick and stone together in their passing.

Strange Way to Grow Old

Autumn for A

for Anthony Schlagel

Strange way to grow old, writing
like every day swimming in the shock
of cold water or counting the stars
or breaking.

Like the body breaks a little.
Craving table, lover, book, music.

Numb with need. Sick with it.
Everything else pushed away.

Words like words, somehow
set together against common sense.
Opening inside it.

Walking at Villa Montalvo

for Norman Fischer

Looking down at my footsteps.
Taking a short walk past the covered
water tank. Over the creek, up through
the abandoned apple orchard.

Thinking about the monk who doesn't
want to know the names of the trees
or of the plants or animals. How he finds
the world in split seconds of not knowing.

Because it's so easy for me to lose my way
thought to thought. To be on the bridge
one moment and sitting at my desk the next.

One day I would like to talk to this monk
who walks between the names we give to things.

Drinking Wine with the Ancestors

All the little pains in my life
don't add up. They've got
so little to say for themselves.

My hands, however, are full
of expressiveness! As if each
finger had been trained
in a different school of the arts.

Life is not a dead-end, one finger says
standing alone on a large empty stage.
Life is its own exit plan, says another finger
stuck in the snow, still miles
from the circus tent.

I don't know where all the fingers
that once touched my run-away body
have run off to.

But I can say a word or two about the wine.

And the book of Chinese poetry
open on the table. And the amateur ballgame
that never ends in the playground
across the street.

And the wine.

Thunderheads

for Megan Simpson and Tom Hall

We sit together on folding chairs
and it's as if we are flying side by side.

Thunderheads running past on feet of cool
hard rain, crossing the Rio Grande Valley.

Their elaborate braids pulled back
into anvil-shaped peaks.

Without mythology, the language
of scientific description, we feel private

as a chain-link fence, as unopened bottles
bumping across uneven ground.

Sitting with hands pressed over eyes, mouths
closed, we remember stories of old people

climbing through a fist-sized hole in the ground,
or through a hollow log, or emerging from a cave

of bluish light. Did their words glow red as rock
and bright as the house we cannot enter?

The Professor's Lament

I left the Humanities Building
and looked up. The sky was bright
and gray. I heard a voice asking,

"What is it that continuously pumps time
in and out of our bodies?"

I knew better than to try to answer
that question. There was too much tension
in my neck and a long band of pain
running elbow to wrist. I knew that
academia was fine. It was just my perspective
that was off with that slight askew
that makes all the difference.

And yet if I believed that everything I needed
was right there in the brain's back pocket,
why did I walk past the last line of academic
buildings, across the sprawling parking lot,
and into the perfect domesticity of an unknown
middleclass neighborhood?

In the chill air, the darkening day,
the gray sky, the last thing I remember
is throwing my pen up in the air
and feeling it bounce off my hand
as I tried to catch it.

A Dream

1.

The puppy-breasted matron scooped her up
in her arms and dropped the shrieking girl
into the well.

The dead girl remembered eating soggy
breakfast cereal and her screams screaming
at her as she fell.

The shrieking girl-child scooped up
and dropped in a well.

2.

She woke startled as if someone standing at
the end of her bed had grabbed the iron
footboard and given it a hard, sharp shake.

What interested her most about the dream
was how her own voice separated from
her body and from her fear as she fell
and became an outside agent attacking
and ridiculing her.

3.

After putting on her kimono she stood
at the window that faces the downtown skyline.
Praying that an earthquake had finally
destroyed her adopted city.

Quilt Writing

For Harryette Mullen

1.

There was the sound of voices
inside the shapes of letters.
A spirit-script continuing
across the ocean. Blue hands,
red coffins, strung like beads
between the shade thrown
by branches and the pain
of what might happen to a black man
or woman stopping for water.

2.

She had turned gray. Turned
to welcome someone from her past.
She had sat down, resting her mind
with a hymn to a folding chair,
a stump, or box.

3.

There was the mixing of mud
behind her eyes. The waiting close
to squares of fabric, strips of colored
cloth, embroidered faces.

Those piercings of difference
which come left-handed, slanted
sideways, as if by accident.

4.

Because the ragged sun
seen on a slave's apron is repeated.
The same saturated purple, the thin
bright red, steal forward
use to use.

Because there is still an image
of that red ragged sun.
Because there is still a land
in which that sun can tell a story.

A piece of glass leaning against the wall
is a door for his or her memory
to mark in passing.

Wilson Wiley Variations, Part Two

The Last Mile Away

Wilson cracks an egg
snips a stalk of rosemary
grinds some coffee

not Wilson but Wiley
or not Wiley but another
superstitious name in the morning

dogs barking across
the neighborhood like a year
spent in the desert

like *What You Say*
crossing the Richmond Bridge
like Wilson Token

Wiley renamed
Jubilant-In-His-Failure
by the foolproof landscape

rhyme is the father of time
W said to W
rhyme can never be mine

he said
breaking bright
and artificial

as the chorus
he dreamt downtown
churched him up

in her arms
the young lover
long haired awkward

her straight hips and
lollygagging tongue
calling God

to lift him higher
than the chorus singing
as broken statues might

we are ruined and beautiful
we are broken and whole
water opening below them

cold cavernous pools
of wilderness below
and all around them

WW wakes to sun
brightened brass bed
sun on top of him

hard as waking to
dreamlessness
or waking backwards

like what someone said
about WW and
she

who got him so
he did not know
where so he was going

waking lost then
and what day
with singing lost

in waking
to wooden floor
hearing batter batter

radio ballgame
the World does not end
in California

nineteen hundred and sixty-two
the year of his birth
claims Wilson Wiley

born between oil fields
and 8 cylinder rock n roll
may one call a question "Father"

may I asks WW beginning
to see red rock desert as fable
his definition derivation deviation

remembered as the crow-black crow
cut from thick-branched pine
is remembered

laughing like hills can laugh
like goats eating every memory
Wilson made

trying to dodge contorted
fig trunks and grim vines
the drunken pop-pop

gunshot and Midwestern
Monotone racing down
the mountain with unseen waves

of music ricocheting
around him
with his grandfather's

shoe-horn
a plastic fiddle and
his waiting

for a simple last-dance dance
the upended wine barrel
its wild white rose

sprawling across the back porch
where WW stands
with a cup of coffee

and a pair of binoculars
overlooking a thumb-sized
garden on the hill called Pot Hill

where goats once jangled
against the sky and above
the cold welcoming Pacific

Italic text: Carole Masso

Gone as Water

Gone as water is Wiley's element. As he enters the city looking for faces that touch the furthest memory of. Passing through layers of wood and brick, dirt and ash and steel. Remembering an explosion that caused an apartment building to collapse.

Wiley found Desire in a street of open windows and summertime voices, the rhapsodic procession of fog entering the city. Found it in short, sharp, mathematical meals.

Gone like everything already happening to Wilson Wiley. Another past tense, fresh and elusive, like the clanging of a streetcar. Gone as Wilson still standing in the rubble, camera and notebook in hand.

Apotheosis of Childhood

Wiley reconstructs the sound of loud music
in a small bedroom. Apotheosis of childhood
becoming landscape. Something to scream
into. Like the dead once-river dribbling to a
stop, between the defunct coffee factory and
the amateur ball park.

Wiley walks down Ninth Street looking
for names the city wears like rough arousal.
Names that dance their sloppy quickness
across corrugated tin, grimy brick, across dull
buzzing metal boxes. Names like *Spunko,
Gone, Orfn*.

Blocks of names and Wiley Wilson confused
to himself says the city repeats itself.
Thousands of cars pushing and pulling
bumper to bass line block after block. A
kind of assembly line Ouroboros, tail lodged
between skyscraper teeth.

Memory's Continuous Ragtime

First there was a mountain, then there was a trailer park, then there was a cemetery. Gone like everybody wants to be gone. Like W wants to escape into W.

The beautiful scarred hills beckoning from the other side of the bridge. Gone like going then going then going. No final ending music. No perfect flower to frame memory's continuous ragtime. Mercy, the itinerant saxophone player. Touch, the chrome-tongued trumpet.

WW left with nothing but *Spunk* and a Name and a fast hand to write with. A home to spit with. To break through a locked door with. A Name like a back seat to be born in. Like an improvisation of highway and tumbleweed. Left with nothing but crickets. Their stories of hunger and patience repeated outside his door.

The Harmonica Kettle's Sad Drone

Home is where the water is, Wilson tells
Wiley. Where the harmonica kettle's
sad drone burns the ear. Home is where
immigrant thoughts collect in corners.
Where the lame wolf drools on the rented
carpet. Where a ragged fiddle tune tricks the
fabulous Wiley into dancing with the literal
Wilson.

Looking out at the late afternoon light,
copper-colored and slanted with the hills,
Wilson remembers wanting to marry the
moon, to sleep with a blackberry bush, to shit
like a crow.

When his eyes return to the kitchen, its black
bars and loud music, its empty refrigerator,
Wiley's backing up with a cigarette and a
warm beer. Reminding Wilson that one day a
billboard will rise over the graveyard, a prison
will circle the city, a mountain will become so
small it will fit in a child's lunch box.

The Edge of Contentment

WW uncurls himself inside her. She who is water, who lives over the hill with the large cement cross, once called Blue Mountain. WW thinks he might cross the bridge north with her. That they might live in the hills overlooking his watery past.

She whose arms enfold, smelling of juniper and avocado oil, whose blue eyes blaze a warm barn out of the fog. WW on the edge of contentment. The air so clear the sky suddenly full of mountains.

She showed him where the creek flowed down 17th street. Where the dunes began their slow westward fall. The city in November thin as pounded gold. As malleable as desire.

When she leaves WW he's sitting in a park on the east slope of a hill overlooking the white-capped bay.

Another Charlie Chaplin Heart Attack

WW watches ragtag builders work the mudflats at low tide, their comic figures emerging from driftwood and detritus.

He follows the images back into his own California. A hunch-backed Chevy sedan limping down the highway. The dream of a child abandoned on a picnic table. Forgotten the way sycamore leaves are after the wind clears the street.

WW waits near the window for blackbirds to fill the sky. He waits in front of the hardware store. Behind the library. Next to the new police station. He sees himself as a young man running full speed and fully into his suffering through a yellow door onto the derrick-strewn highway. Another Charlie Chaplin heart attack gasping for the Mexican flower girl to reappear, to arouse him with roses.

The Chevy sits on uneven blacktop, gently rocking back and forth. The Airstream silver and star-bright behind it. Like a comet returning every time WW closes his eyes.

The Vat-Like Valley

Landscapes spiral away as if seen in a rearview mirror, from inside a dark compartment. Spring-loaded fields of corn. High-pitched acres of suburban monotony. Receding as speed stabilizes, becomes part of the family.

Lights cascade over the Grapevine, into the vat-like valley. Flooding the desert once thick with elk and geese. WW runs right into the middle-maze of America. Stranded in another kind of desert.

Charlie C., Mr. Black and White Chaplin, calling through the bicycle-soundtrack can't reach WW, who sits in the playground near the chain-link fence, watching hospital-clouds rush across the valley and crash into mountains east.

So little rain. So much geological change inside the body. As if a glacier named Wilson Wiley were grinding slowly North to South. Or retreating slowly South to North. As a church inside the body might.

WW follows maps made from fragments of conversation, discovers two separate lakes.

One massive concrete dam towering over the valley. One shallow sprawling lake drained. Now entering WW the way flocks of birds unbalance the sky.

A Book Called Forgetting

Wilson Wiley writing it all down in a book called Forgetting. Sitting at the black table with the blinds open. The tended-to sycamores in the park across the street, their yellowing leaves still months away from bare branches.

Waiting with the owl and spider, the mouse and pigeon. It is my intention, says Wilson Wiley, my escape, says he, to play both tortoise and hare. To cut both circle and straight line.

As if to speak and to follow silence back through the pages. To where a tall man pushes a stroller down the boardwalk. Having brought WW there to watch the water change color. The water not the sky.

About the Author

Thoreau Lovell is a poet and fiction writer, originally from Fresno, California. He now lives in Berkeley with his wife and two daughters. He is the author of a book of prose poems, *Public Servant* (Toehold Books) and a book of poetry, *Amnesia's Diary* (Ex Nihilo Press). He worked for many years in the J. Paul Leonard Library at San Francisco State University, primarily as an administrator responsible for technology and collection access. A former editor at *Five Fingers Review/Press*, he currently is part of the Wet Cement Press collective. For more information visit his website *ThoreauLovell.com*.

Wet Cement Press Titles

Series 1

My Dog, Me (novel), Anthony Schlagel
ISBN 978-1-7324369-3-0 (2019)

Saraswati's Lament (poetry), Barbara Roether
ISBN 978-1-7324369-0-9 (2019)

Synonym for Home (poetry), Michelle Murphy
ISBN 978-1-7324369-2-3 (2019)

Wilson Wiley Variations (poetry), Thoreau Lovell
ISBN 978-1-7324369-1-6 (2019)

www.ingramcontent.com/pod-product-compliance
Lightning Source LLC
Chambersburg PA
CBHW021638080526
44584CB00015BA/1523